Teacups & Gingerbread

A Kitchen Journal

This kitchen journal belongs to:

____

____

Gooseberry Patch
149 Johnson Drive
Department BOOK
Delaware, OH 43015

1·800·85·GOOSE
1-800·854·6673

Copyright 1995, **Gooseberry Patch** 0-9632978-4-8
Second Printing, October, 1998

How To Subscribe

Would you like to receive
"A Country Store in Your Mailbox®?"
For a 2-year subscription to our 88-page
Gooseberry Patch catalog, simply send $3.00 to:

Gooseberry Patch
149 Johnson Drive
Department BOOK
Delaware, OH 43015

TABLE of CONTENTS

My
Kitchen
WISH LIST

snug as a bug in a rug

Start a whimsical collection...

of old cutting boards in all shapes and sizes!

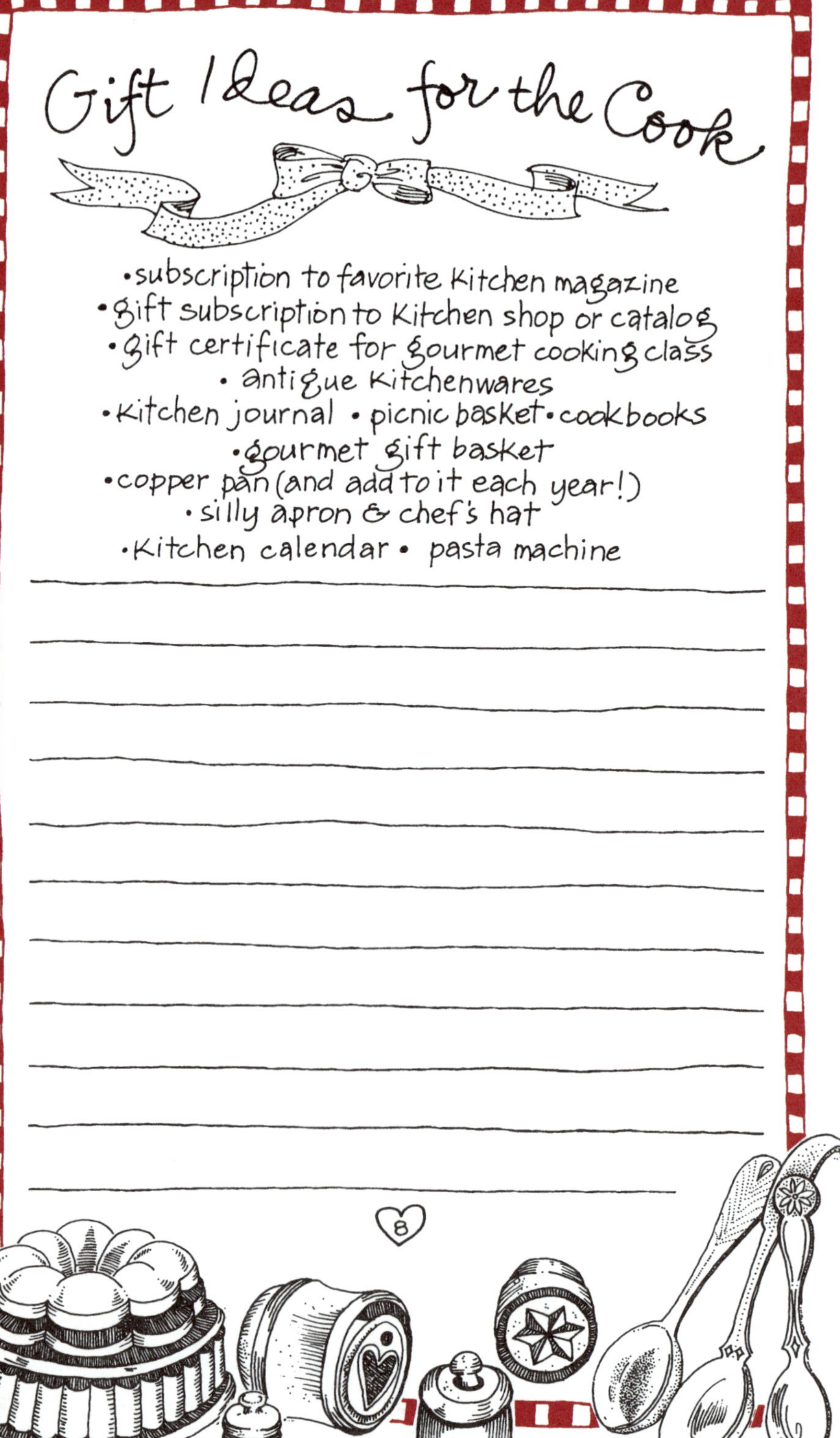

Gift Ideas for the Cook

- subscription to favorite kitchen magazine
- gift subscription to kitchen shop or catalog
- gift certificate for gourmet cooking class
- antique kitchenwares
- kitchen journal • picnic basket • cookbooks
- gourmet gift basket
- copper pan (and add to it each year!)
- silly apron & chef's hat
- kitchen calendar • pasta machine

NOTES
from a
country
kitchen

When rolling out sugar cookies, roll out on powdered sugar...

...instead of flour. It works just as well and adds to the flavor just a bit more.

A pretty serving platter...
Pam's Jam
Elly's Jelly
...can double as a breakfast tray

Come ye thankful people come;
Raise the song of Harvest-home;
All is safely gathered in;
Ere the winter storms begin.

HENRY ALFORD

Equivalents

3 teaspoons = 1 Tablespoon
4 Tablespoons = ¼ cup
1 stick of butter = ½ cup
1 pound of brown sugar = 2 ¼ cup (packed)
1 pound powdered sugar = 4 cups (sifted)
8 egg whites = about 1c. (good to know for making angel cakes!)
8 egg yolks = about ½ cup
1 cup raw rice = 3-4 cups cooked
1 medium lemon yields 2-3 Tbs. juice
1 pound seedless raisins = 3 cups
2 oz. chocolate chips = ⅓ cup
6 oz. chocolate chips = 1 cup

PLANNING

... my country kitchen

Make your kitchen
warm and inviting
with hanging baskets,
shiny copper pots and pans,
fragrant bundles of herbs and
good smells coming from the oven!

Antique cupboards, pie safes, and servers provide additional storage and lend a warm, inviting touch to your kitchen

21

Candles in the kitchen are a must, and the fragrances are delicious....cinnamon, spiced apple...

blueberry, strawberry, vanilla, just to name a few!

I'm as warm as toast

My Favorite Kitchen Collectibles

A great place to find old farm
baskets, crocks, wooden totes,
and kitchen gadgets is a
flea market!

The·Well-Stocked· P·A·N·T·R·Y·

~A Short List to Get You Started~

Flour, Sugar, Salt - of course!
Spaghetti · Noodles
Rice · Raisins
Chicken Broth
Canned Beans · Tuna
Olive Oil
Biscuit Mix
Chocolate Chips
Peanut Butter

MY FAVORITE
Recipes

Remember Aunt Bea's Kitchen, with apple pie cooling on the windowsill?

If you take the last of anything from

a plate, you have to kiss the cook.

Too many cooks...

...spoil the broth.

There are
few hours
in life
more
agreeable
than
afternoon
tea.

Henry James

cooking... with women, a weapon to catch men by the stomach...

...and watch it grow
with the years.
Anonymous

...The most favorite room of the house...

...is the kitchen...the heart of the home!

Instead of making
all your cookies
from scratch,
buy a mix
or slice-and-bakes.

Assemble lots
of sugars,
sparkles, and
colored icings
and have fun!

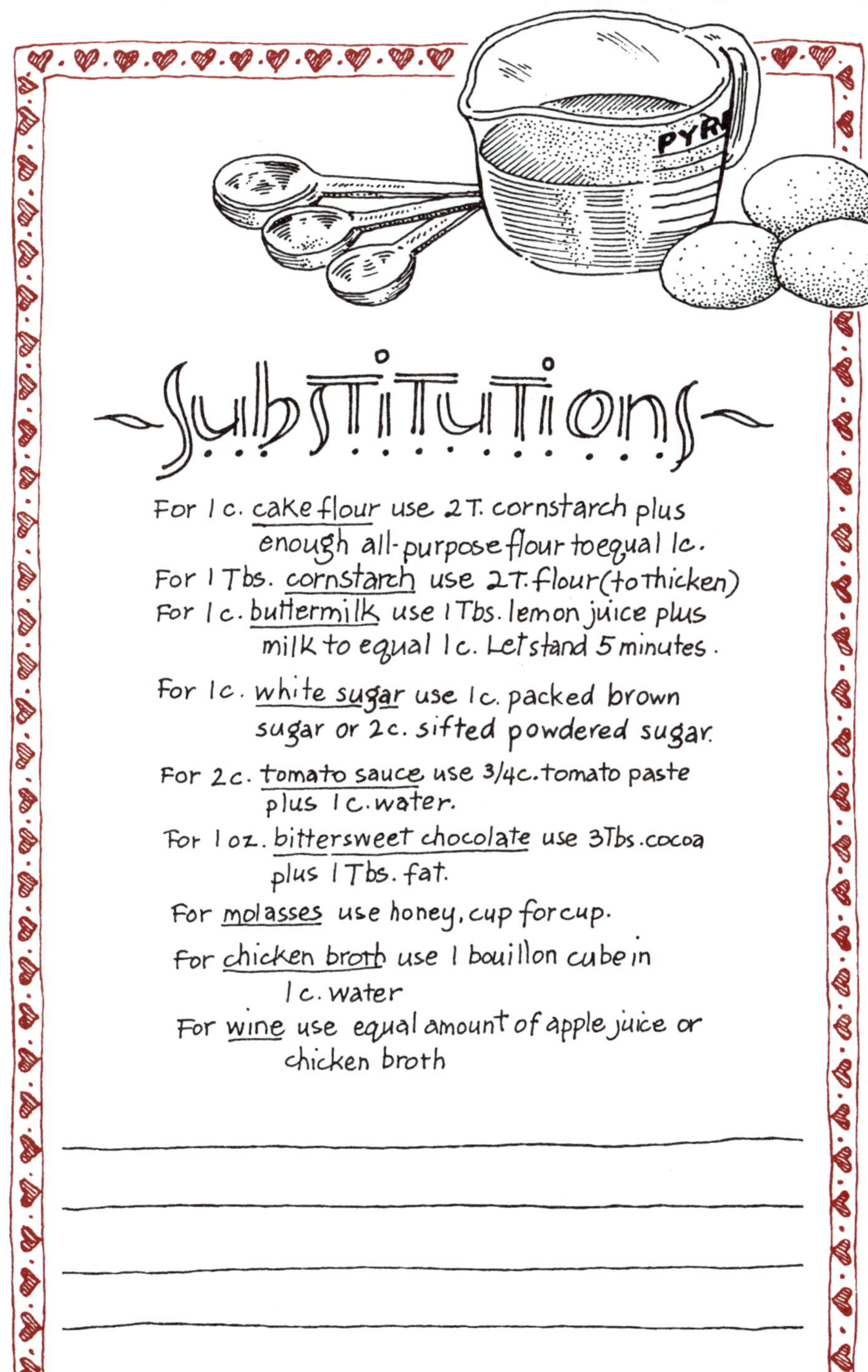

~Substitutions~

For 1 c. <u>cake flour</u> use 2 T. cornstarch plus
    enough all-purpose flour to equal 1 c.
For 1 Tbs. <u>cornstarch</u> use 2 T. flour (to thicken)
For 1 c. <u>buttermilk</u> use 1 Tbs. lemon juice plus
    milk to equal 1 c. Let stand 5 minutes.
For 1 c. <u>white sugar</u> use 1 c. packed brown
    sugar or 2 c. sifted powdered sugar.
For 2 c. <u>tomato sauce</u> use 3/4 c. tomato paste
    plus 1 c. water.
For 1 oz. <u>bittersweet chocolate</u> use 3 Tbs. cocoa
    plus 1 Tbs. fat.
For <u>molasses</u> use honey, cup for cup.
For <u>chicken broth</u> use 1 bouillon cube in
    1 c. water
For <u>wine</u> use equal amount of apple juice or
    chicken broth

Table Settings

GREAT IDEAS for SPECIAL OCCASIONS

It's fun to put together a ________________ set of mismatched china. Choose a particular shade of blue and even a hodge-podge of designs will look good.

47

"Frost" oranges, lemons, limes, apples, and grapes for garnishes and centerpieces...

Simply brush fresh fruit with beaten egg white, then roll in sugar.

49

Make your
pumpkin pie
something special.

With pie dough scraps, cut out
autumn leaves, hearts, or
stars and place on top
of pie. Bake
as directed.

Decorate
a kitchen tree
with cookies...
tiny gnomes, heart-
in-hands, or gingerbread
men look great and smell
delicious. So homey, too!

Tried & True Menus for Special Occasions

A soup tureen can double...
as a centerpiece filled with fresh flowers

"Get off my case, mom!"
More "cases" have been heard at the kitchen table . . .

...than in all the courts combined.

Invite a friend over for "tea for two". Serve herbal tea and pretty heart-shaped cucumber and cream cheese sandwiches, sit at...

The table

and talk, talk, talk! ©59

Bake apples
on a tray in a
slow oven (200°)
all day and
your country kitchen
will smell wonderful!

Cookie cutters are fun to decorate with, too...
show them off in a big wooden bowl, line them...

62

...up on your kitchen windowsill ~
or use them as napkin rings!

Herb Chart

WHAT GOES WITH WHAT?

Here are some ideas. Jot down your own inspirations.

Fish - Dill, parsley, thyme
Beef - Bay leaf, pepper, chili powder
Pork - Ginger, garlic, cumin, oregano
Chicken ~ Rosemary, tarragon, thyme
Lamb - Mint, rosemary, garlic
Ham ~ Cloves, dry mustard
Eggs ~ Chives, parsley, basil
Tomatoes - Basil, cumin
Spaghetti sauce ~ oregano, marjoram, basil
Fruit - Mint, cinnamon, coriander

my kitchen MEMORIES

A loving gift for your child...assemble a recipe box filled with your favorite family recipes.

Add funny little sayings... truly a box full of memories.

Enjoy your embroidered tablecloths from Grandma...don't hide them in a drawer. And remember, pretty dish towels make wonderful...

68

...napkins and cover your entire lap!

·Tips·and·Ideas·that·WARM·your·soul·

A favorite winter cozy…

Gooseberry

...from the Kitchen is cocoa. Add whipped cream, a candy cane, or cinnamon stick for extra flavor.

Make your country kitchen cozy
by simmering whole cloves, cinnamon
sticks, orange rind, and allspice. This
"potion" can be used
over and over again.

Gifts
from my kitchen

china or glass plates at...

74 During the year, purchase pretty but inexpensive

flea markets, garage sales and estate sales. Use them for giving as gifts from your kitchen.

Fill kitchen gift baskets
with gourmet treats,
cookbooks, journals,
towels, wooden spoons,
and cookie cutters.

A must-have for every country kitchen is a peg rack for hanging coats, hats, candles, herbs, baskets, whatever!

Get together with friends over breakfast!....

... Simplicity is the key...muffins, fruit, tea, chilled juice and fresh flowers!

fruit, tea, chilled juice and fresh flowers!

BLOOPS AND BLUNDERS

The kitchen is
where memories
happen... successes,
~~fai~~lures, and just plain fun. Keep your camera handy!

warranty information

Let a gentle spring shower freshen your dusty baskets... removes all the cobwebs and does wonders for lifting your spirits! Allow to air dry in a shady spot.

Galvanized buckets
and tubs make
great containers for holding
ice and cold beverages.
Festive!

the best KITCHEN CATALOGS • SHOPS • & COOKBOOKS

If
you
can't
stand
the heat,
get out
of
the
kitchen.

1788
89

there's no
better smell to wake up to than...
coffee

...fresh brewed coffee!

Telephone
numbers
I frequently call

Police Department _______________________

Fire Department _______________________

Doctor _______________________

Dentist _______________________

Hospital _______________________

Poison Control _______________________

School _______________________

Babysitter _______________________

Plumber _______________________

Electrician _______________________

Bank _______________________

Other _______________________

____

____

____

____

____

We've cooked up a whole collection of Gooseberry Patch® books!

Have a taste for more? Call us toll-free at
1-800-854-6673

We'll send you our latest catalog filled with snowmen, Santas, ornaments, candles, cookie cutters, gourmet goodies, salt-glazed pottery collectibles and MORE...including our best-selling cookbooks!

Phone us:
1·800·854·6673

Fax us:
1·740·363·7225

Visit our website:
www.gooseberrypatch.com

Send us your favorite recipe!

and the memory that makes it special for you! * We're putting together a brand new **Gooseberry Patch** cookbook, and you're invited to participate. If we select your recipe, your name will appear right along with it...and you'll receive a FREE copy of the book! Mail to:

Vickie & Jo Ann
Gooseberry Patch, Dept. BOOK
P.O. Box 190
Delaware, Ohio 43015

*Please help us by including the number of servings and all other necessary information!

DIAGNOSTIC CRITERIA

FROM

DSM-III-R

Table of Contents

Introduction

One of the most important features of DSM-III-R is its provision of diagnostic criteria to improve the reliability of diagnostic judgments. With this approach, the clinician's task is twofold: to determine the presence or absence of specific clinical features, and then to use the criteria provided as guidelines for making the diagnosis. For quick reference, the clinician may wish to have available a small manual that contains only the classification, the diagnostic criteria, decision trees that aid in understanding the organization of the classification, an abbreviated symptom-based index, and alphabetic and numeric listings of the diagnoses and codes—hence, this Reference to the Diagnostic Criteria from DSM-III-R, which we affectionately call the "Mini-D."

Proper use of this manual requires familiarity with the description of the diagnostic categories and with the glossary of definitions of technical terms contained in DSM-III-R.

Robert L. Spitzer, M.D.
Chair, Work Group to Revise DSM-III

Janet B.W. Williams, D.S.W.
Text Editor

Cautionary Statement

The specified diagnostic criteria for each mental disorder are offered as guidelines for making diagnoses, since it has been demonstrated that the use of such criteria enhances agreement among clinicians and investigators. The proper use of these criteria requires specialized clinical training that provides both a body of knowledge and clinical skills.

These diagnostic criteria reflect a consensus of current formulations of evolving knowledge in our field but do not encompass all the conditions that may be legitimate objects of treatment or research efforts.

The purpose of DSM-III-R is to provide clear descriptions of diagnostic categories in order to enable clinicians and investigators to diagnose, communicate about, study, and treat the various mental disorders. It is to be understood that inclusion here, for clinical and research purposes, of a diagnostic category such as Pathological Gambling or Pedophilia does not imply that the condition meets legal or other nonmedical criteria for what constitutes mental disease, mental disorder, or mental disability. The clinical and scientific considerations involved in categorization of these conditions as mental disorders may not be wholly relevant to legal judgments, for example, that take into account such issues as individual responsibility, disability determination, and competency.

DSM-III-R Classification

DSM-III-R Classification: Axes I and II Categories and Codes

All official DSM-III-R codes are included in ICD-9-CM. Codes followed by a * are used for more than one DSM-III-R diagnosis or sub-type in order to maintain compatibility with ICD-9-CM.

A long dash following a diagnostic term indicates the need for a fifth digit subtype or other qualifying term.

Numbers in parentheses are page numbers.

The term *specify* following the name of some diagnostic categories indicates qualifying terms that clinicians may wish to add in parentheses after the name of the disorder.

NOS = Not Otherwise Specified

The current severity of a disorder may be specified after the diagnosis as:

currently
mild ⎤ meets
moderate ⎦— diagnostic
severe ⎦ criteria

in partial remission
  (or residual state)
in complete remission

DISORDERS USUALLY FIRST EVIDENT IN INFANCY, CHILDHOOD, OR ADOLESCENCE

DEVELOPMENTAL DISORDERS

Note: These are coded on Axis II.

Mental Retardation (47)

317.00	Mild mental retardation
318.00	Moderate mental retardation
318.10	Severe mental retardation
318.20	Profound mental retardation
319.00	Unspecified mental retardation

Pervasive Developmental Disorders (49)

299.00	Autistic disorder
	Specify if childhood onset
299.80	Pervasive developmental disorder NOS

Specific Developmental Disorders (52)

Academic skills disorders (52)

315.10	Developmental arithmetic disorder
315.80	Developmental expressive writing disorder
315.00	Developmental reading disorder

Language and speech disorders (53)

315.39	Developmental articulation disorder
315.31*	Developmental expressive language disorder
315.31*	Developmental receptive language disorder

Motor skills disorder (55)

315.40	Developmental coordination disorder
315.90*	Specific developmental disorder NOS

Other Developmental Disorders (56)

315.90*   Developmental disorder NOS

Disruptive Behavior Disorders (56)

314.01   Attention-deficit hyperactivity disorder

            Conduct disorder,
312.20   group type
312.00   solitary aggressive type
312.90   undifferentiated type
313.81   Oppositional defiant disorder

Anxiety Disorders of Childhood or Adolescence (61)

309.21   Separation anxiety disorder
313.21   Avoidant disorder of childhood or
            adolescence
313.00   Overanxious disorder

Eating Disorders (63)

307.10   Anorexia nervosa
307.51   Bulimia nervosa
307.52   Pica
307.53   Rumination disorder of infancy
307.50   Eating disorder NOS

Gender Identity Disorders (65)

302.60   Gender identity disorder of childhood
302.50   Transsexualism
            Specify sexual history: asexual, homo-
            sexual, heterosexual, unspecified

302.85*   Gender identity disorder of adolescence
                or adulthood, nontranssexual type
                    Specify sexual history: asexual, homo-
                    sexual, heterosexual, unspecified
302.85*   Gender identity disorder NOS

Tic Disorders (68)

307.23   Tourette's disorder
307.22   Chronic motor or vocal tic disorder
307.21   Transient tic disorder
                    Specify: single episode or recurrent
307.20   Tic disorder NOS

Elimination Disorders (70)

307.70   Functional encopresis
                    Specify: primary or secondary type
307.60   Functional enuresis
                    Specify: primary or secondary type
                    Specify: nocturnal only, diurnal only,
                    nocturnal and diurnal

Speech Disorders Not Elsewhere Classified (72)

307.00*   Cluttering
307.00*   Stuttering

Other Disorders of Infancy, Childhood, or Adolescence (72)

313.23   Elective mutism
313.82   Identity disorder
313.89   Reactive attachment disorder of infancy or
                early childhood
307.30   Stereotypy/habit disorder
314.00   Undifferentiated attention-deficit disorder

ORGANIC MENTAL DISORDERS (77)

Dementias Arising in the Senium and Presenium (84)

Primary degenerative dementia of the Alzheimer type, senile onset

290.30	with delirium
290.20	with delusions
290.21	with depression
290.00*	uncomplicated

(Note: code 331.00 Alzheimer's disease on Axis III)

Code in fifth digit: 1 = with delirium, 2 = with delusions, 3 = with depression, 0* = uncomplicated.

290.1x Primary degenerative dementia of the Alzheimer type, presenile onset, _______ (Note: code 331.00 Alzheimer's disease on Axis III)

290.4x Multi-infarct dementia, _______

290.00* Senile dementia NOS
Specify etiology on Axis III if known

290.10* Presenile dementia NOS
Specify etiology on Axis III if known (e.g., Pick's disease, Jakob-Creutzfeldt disease)

Psychoactive Substance-Induced Organic Mental Disorders (86)

Alcohol (86)

303.00	intoxication
291.40	idiosyncratic intoxication

291.00	withdrawal delirium
291.30	hallucinosis
291.10	amnestic disorder
291.20	Dementia associated with alcoholism

Amphetamine or similarly acting
sympathomimetic (89)

305.70*	intoxication
292.00*	withdrawal
292.81*	delirium
292.11*	delusional disorder

Caffeine (91)

305.90*	intoxication

Cannabis (91)

305.20*	intoxication
292.11*	delusional disorder

Cocaine (92)

305.60*	intoxication
292.00*	withdrawal
292.81*	delirium
292.11*	delusional disorder

Hallucinogen (94)

305.30*	hallucinosis
292.11*	delusional disorder
292.84*	mood disorder
292.89*	Posthallucinogen perception disorder

Inhalant (96)

305.90*	intoxication

Nicotine (97)

292.00*	withdrawal

Opioid (97)

305.50*	intoxication
292.00*	withdrawal

Phencyclidine (PCP) or similarly acting
arylcyclohexylamine (98)

305.90*	intoxication
292.81*	delirium
292.11*	delusional disorder
292.84*	mood disorder
292.90*	organic mental disorder NOS

Sedative, hypnotic, or anxiolytic (101)

305.40*	intoxication
292.00*	Uncomplicated sedative, hypnotic, or anxiolytic withdrawal
292.00*	withdrawal delirium
292.83*	amnestic disorder

Other or unspecified psychoactive
substance (103)

305.90*	intoxication
292.00*	withdrawal
292.81*	delirium
292.82*	dementia
292.83*	amnestic disorder
292.11*	delusional disorder
292.12	hallucinosis
292.84*	mood disorder
292.89*	anxiety disorder
292.89*	personality disorder
292.90*	organic mental disorder NOS

Organic Mental Disorders associated with Axis III physical disorders or conditions, or whose etiology is unknown. (77)

293.00	Delirium (77)
294.10	Dementia (78)
294.00	Amnestic disorder (80)
293.81	Organic delusional disorder (81)
293.82	Organic hallucinosis (81)

293.83	Organic mood disorder (81)
	Specify: manic, depressed, mixed
294.80*	Organic anxiety disorder (82)
310.10	Organic personality disorder (82)
	Specify if explosive type
294.80*	Organic mental disorder NOS

PSYCHOACTIVE SUBSTANCE USE DISORDERS (107)

Alcohol
303.90   dependence
305.00   abuse

Amphetamine or similarly acting
sympathomimetic
304.40   dependence
305.70*   abuse

Cannabis
304.30   dependence
305.20*   abuse

Cocaine
304.20   dependence
305.60*   abuse

Hallucingoen
304.50*   dependence
305.30*   abuse

Inhalant
304.60   dependence
305.90*   abuse

Nicotine
305.10   dependence

Opioid
304.00   dependence
305.50*   abuse

Phencyclidine (PCP) or similarly acting arylcyclohexylamine

304.50*	dependence
305.90*	abuse

Sedative, hypnotic, or anxiolytic

304.10	dependence
305.40*	abuse

304.90*	Polysubstance dependence (110)
304.90*	Psychoactive substance dependence NOS
305.90*	Psychoactive substance abuse NOS

SCHIZOPHRENIA (113)

Code in fifth digit: 1 = subchronic, 2 = chronic, 3 = subchronic with acute exacerbation, 4 = chronic with acute exacerbation, 5 = in remission, 0 = unspecified.

Schizophrenia

295.2x	catatonic, _________
295.1x	disorganized, _________
295.3x	paranoid, _________
	Specify if stable type
295.9x	undifferentiated, _________
295.6x	residual, _________

Specify if late onset

DELUSIONAL (PARANOID) DISORDER (119)

297.10	Delusional (Paranoid) disorder

Specify type: erotomanic
grandiose
jealous
persecutory
somatic
unspecified

PSYCHOTIC DISORDERS NOT ELSEWHERE CLASSIFIED (121)

298.80   Brief reactive psychosis
295.40   Schizophreniform disorder
           Specify: without good prognostic features or with good prognostic features
295.70   Schizoaffective disorder
           Specify: bipolar type or depressive type
297.30   Induced psychotic disorder
298.90   Psychotic disorder NOS (Atypical psychosis)

MOOD DISORDERS (125)

Code current state of Major Depression and Bipolar Disorder in fifth digit:
  1 = mild
  2 = moderate
  3 = severe, without psychotic features
  4 = with psychotic features (*specify* mood-congruent or mood-incongruent)
  5 = in partial remission
  6 = in full remission
  0 = unspecified

For major depressive episodes, *specify* if chronic and *specify* if melancholic type.

For Bipolar Disorder, Bipolar Disorder NOS, Recurrent Major Depression, and Depressive Disorder NOS, *specify* if seasonal pattern.

Bipolar Disorders (132)

       Bipolar disorder
296.6x   mixed, _________
296.4x   manic, _________
296.5x   depressed, _________

301.13	Cyclothymia
296.70	Bipolar disorder NOS

Depressive Disorders (135)

	Major Depression
296.2x	single episode, ________
296.3x	recurrent, ________
300.40	Dysthymia (or Depressive neurosis)
	Specify: primary or secondary type
	Specify: early or late onset
311.00	Depressive disorder NOS

ANXIETY DISORDERS (or Anxiety and Phobic Neuroses) (139)

	Panic disorder
300.21	with agoraphobia
	Specify current severity of agoraphobic avoidance
	Specify current severity of panic attacks
300.01	without agoraphobia
	Specify: current severity of panic attacks
300.22	Agoraphobia without history of panic disorder
	Specify with or without limited symptom attacks
300.23	Social phobia
	Specify if generalized type
300.29	Simple phobia
300.30	Obsessive compulsive disorder (or Obsessive compulsive neurosis)
309.89	Post-traumatic stress disorder
	Specify if delayed onset
300.02	Generalized anxiety disorder
300.00	Anxiety disorder NOS

SOMATOFORM DISORDERS (151)

300.70*	Body dysmorphic disorder
300.11	Conversion disorder (or Hysterical neurosis, conversion type)
	Specify: single episode or recurrent
300.70*	Hypochondriasis (or Hypochondriacal neurosis)
300.81	Somatization disorder
307.80	Somatoform pain disorder
300.70*	Undifferentiated somatoform disorder
300.70*	Somatoform disorder NOS

DISSOCIATIVE DISORDERS (or Hysterical Neuroses, Dissociative Type) (157)

300.14	Multiple personality disorder
300.13	Psychogenic fugue
300.12	Psychogenic amnesia
300.60	Depersonalization disorder (or Depersonalization neurosis)
300.15	Dissociative disorder NOS

SEXUAL DISORDERS (161)

Paraphilias (161)

302.40	Exhibitionism
302.81	Fetishism
302.89	Frotteurism
302.20	Pedophilia
	Specify: same sex, opposite sex, same and opposite sex
	Specify if limited to incest
	Specify: exclusive type or nonexclusive type
302.83	Sexual masochism
302.84	Sexual sadism

302.30	Transvestic fetishism
302.82	Voyeurism
302.90*	Paraphilia NOS

Sexual Dysfunctions (164)

Specify: psychogenic only, or psychogenic and biogenic (Note: If biogenic only, code on Axis III)
Specify: lifelong or acquired
Specify: generalized or situational

Sexual desire disorders

302.71	Hypoactive sexual desire disorder
302.79	Sexual aversion disorder

Sexual arousal disorders

302.72*	Female sexual arousal disorder
302.72*	Male erectile disorder

Orgasm disorders

302.73	Inhibited female orgasm
302.74	Inhibited male orgasm
302.75	Premature ejaculation

Sexual pain disorders

302.76	Dyspareunia
306.51	Vaginismus
302.70	Sexual dysfunction NOS

Other Sexual Disorders (168)

302.90*	Sexual disorder NOS

SLEEP DISORDERS (171)

Dyssomnias (171)

Insomnia disorder

307.42*	related to another mental disorder (non-organic)

780.50*	related to known organic factor
307.42*	Primary insomnia
	Hypersomnia disorder
307.44	related to another mental disorder (non-organic)
780.50*	related to a known organic factor
780.54	Primary hypersomnia
307.45	Sleep-wake schedule disorder

    Specify: advanced or delayed phase type, disorganized type, frequently changing type

Other dyssomnias

307.40*	Dyssomnia NOS

Parasomnias (175)

307.47	Dream anxiety disorder (Nightmare disorder)
307.46*	Sleep terror disorder
307.46*	Sleepwalking disorder
307.40*	Parasomnia NOS

FACTITIOUS DISORDERS (177)

	Factitious disorder
301.51	with physical symptoms
300.16	with psychological symptoms
300.19	Factitious disorder NOS

IMPULSE CONTROL DISORDERS NOT ELSEWHERE CLASSIFIED (179)

312.34	Intermittent explosive disorder
312.32	Kleptomania
312.31	Pathological gambling
312.33	Pyromania
312.39*	Trichotillomania
312.39*	Impulse control disorder NOS

ADJUSTMENT DISORDER (183)

	Adjustment disorder
309.24	with anxious mood
309.00	with depressed mood
309.30	with disturbance of conduct
309.40	with mixed disturbance of emotions and conduct
309.28	with mixed emotional features
309.82	with physical complaints
309.83	with withdrawal
309.23	with work (or academic) inhibition
309.90	Adjustment disorder NOS

PSYCHOLOGICAL FACTORS AFFECTING PHYSICAL CONDITION (187)

316.00   Psychological factors affecting physical condition
Specify physical condition on Axis III

PERSONALITY DISORDERS (189)

Note: These are coded on Axis II.

Cluster A (189)

301.00	Paranoid
301.20	Schizoid
301.22	Schizotypal

Cluster B (192)

301.70	Antisocial
301.83	Borderline
301.50	Histrionic
301.81	Narcissistic

Cluster C (197)

301.82	Avoidant
301.60	Dependent
301.40	Obsessive compulsive
301.84	Passive aggressive
301.90	Personality disorder NOS

V CODES FOR CONDITIONS NOT ATTRIBUTABLE TO A MENTAL DISORDER THAT ARE A FOCUS OF ATTENTION OR TREATMENT (203)

V62.30	Academic problem
V71.01	Adult antisocial behavior

V40.00	Borderline intellectual functioning (Note: This is coded on Axis II.)

V71.02	Childhood or adolescent antisocial behavior
V65.20	Malingering
V61.10	Marital problem
V15.81	Noncompliance with medical treatment
V62.20	Occupational problem
V61.20	Parent-child problem
V62.81	Other interpersonal problem
V61.80	Other specified family circumstances
V62.89	Phase of life problem or other life circumstance problem
V62.82	Uncomplicated bereavement

ADDITIONAL CODES (209)

300.90	Unspecified mental disorder (non-psychotic)
V71.09*	No diagnosis or condition on Axis I

799.90*   Diagnosis or condition deferred on Axis I

V71.09*	No diagnosis or condition on Axis II
799.90*	Diagnosis or condition deferred on Axis II

MULTIAXIAL SYSTEM

Axis I   Clinical Syndromes
V Codes

Axis II   Developmental Disorders
Personality Disorders

Axis III   Physical Disorders and Conditions

Axis IV   Severity of Psychosocial Stressors

Axis V   Global Assessment of Functioning

Severity of Psychosocial Stressors Scale: Adults

See p. 33 for instructions on how to use this scale.

Code	Term	Examples of stressors	
		Acute events	**Enduring circumstances**
1	**None**	No acute events that may be relevant to the disorder	No enduring circumstances that may be relevant to the disorder
2	**Mild**	Broke up with boyfriend or girlfriend; started or graduated from school; child left home	Family arguments; job dissatisfaction; residence in high-crime neighborhood
3	**Moderate**	Marriage; marital separation; loss of job; retirement; miscarriage	Marital discord; serious financial problems; trouble with boss; being a single parent
4	**Severe**	Divorce; birth of first child	Unemployment; poverty
5	**Extreme**	Death of spouse; serious physical illness diagnosed; victim of rape	Serious chronic illness in self or child; ongoing physical or sexual abuse
6	**Catastrophic**	Death of child; suicide of spouse; devastating natural disaster	Captivity as hostage; concentration camp experience
0	**Inadequate information, or no change in condition**		

20